Build to Last Workbook

Build to Last Workbook

A Step-by-step Guide to Long-term Network Marketing Success

Keith Callahan

Published by Ten Hands Publishing

PO Box 172
Sherborn, Massachusetts 01770

ISBN: 978-0-578-50952-5

This workbook is dedicated to you,

the next leader in network marketing.

I believe in you and know you have what it takes.

Now make it happen.

Table of Contents

The Purpose of Your *Build to Last Workbook*

When I wrote *Build to Last,* I wasn't sure how it would be received. I felt this way because I wasn't teaching you about shiny objects, quick fixes, or overnight success. Instead I focused on what real personal development looks like, what it really takes to achieve success at the highest levels in our industry, and the need for you – a network marketing professional – to grow into a leadership role. So much of *Build to Last* addresses who you must become rather than what you have to do. That's not easy work, and I wasn't sure you would embrace it.

Your feedback has been overwhelming clear, though. You are more than ready to put in the real work necessary to receive all the benefits our amazing industry has to offer.

Immediately after launching *Build to Last*, two things happened:

1. Leaders messaged me with positive feedback about the book and to let me know they were recommending it to all their leaders.
2. Leaders shared with me that they were setting up study groups to go through the principles in *Build to Last.*

Turns out that people in our industry were craving the philosophy and teachings in *Build to Last.* This is exciting and gratifying for me because your natural next step is to go to work on the principles – to BECOME a leader, not just passively consume information.

This workbook is designed to help you become what you read about in *Build to Last* by taking massive action.

Before you begin, here are a few notes on the process.

Group or Individual Work

Although you can productively work through the steps alone, to get the most out of this workbook, I recommend going through it in a group setting. If I were to introduce *Build to Last* to my downline, I might begin with one big virtual meeting, then have people break into smaller groups of five to ten for weekly module meetings.

One Module Each Week for 13 Weeks

There are 13 modules in the workbook. I recommend going through one module a week, working through each of the six sections:

- READ – Either reread the corresponding chapter in *Build to Last* or read the abridged version in the workbook.
- GOAL – This is the outcome you are looking to achieve upon completing the weekly work in the module.
- DO – These action steps expand upon those recommended in *Build to Last.* Give yourself one to two hours to do this work at the beginning of each week.
- ACCELERATE – The daily mantra, meditation, reflection, and journaling practices offered here make a real difference. Give any or all of them a try, even if they're unfamiliar to you. The mantras and meditations change each week to support your goal for the module. Evaluate their effectiveness after at least a dedicated week of using these tools.
- DISCUSS – These are discussion topics for a group at the end of the week/module. Consider them even if you're not doing the *Build to Last Workbook* in a group.
- TRACK – At the end of each module, you'll find a habit tracker and space to record your progress and the insights that arise during your evening reflection, one for each of seven days.

The Work You Put In = The Result You Get Out

You can do as little or as much of the work of building to last as you choose, of course. Your results will depend on what you put into the step-by-step work.

As you move through the workbook modules, it's also necessary to stay focused on the daily activities of your business: keep presenting your product, program, opportunity, or service to others, and keep following up with them. You can track your progress in the TRACK section.

Visualize Your Highest Good

When I start mentoring new people, they're often unfamiliar with the practice of visualization, a tool used by high achievers in all arenas (and supported by research). Visualization is simply seeing what you want *in your mind* before it comes into being. I'm a testament to visualization – and consistent hard work. My vision was to make $1 million a year as a network marketing professional. Crazy goal because I had never made more than $100,000 a year in my life. I had no idea *how* it was possible, but somewhere inside of me, I knew it was. I focused on seeing it, focused on believing it, and eventually came to *know* it was going to happen. That knowing seemed to act like a magnetic power attracting success to me.

In each module of this workbook, I invite you to use visualizing in your morning meditation to focus on seeing and experiencing and believing in the person you want to become and the success you want to create. First your vision gets into your heart and soul, and then it starts appearing in your life.

Second Half of the Book

As you'll see, Modules 8 through 13 are designed to support you once you have people – potential leaders – in your team or downline. If you don't, then work though Module 7, go out and find people to work with, and come back to the workbook.

You've got this! You can become a leader of leaders in a successful business that's built to last. Turn the page, and let's get started.

Keith Callahan

Module 1
BUILD TO LAST AND LEADERSHIP

The function of leadership is to produce more leaders, not more followers.
— Ralph Nader

GOAL

To shift from seeing yourself as a distributor for your parent company to being the CEO of your own business.

READ

Our industry has two distinct types of leader:

leaders of followers
and
leaders of leaders.

Leadership expert John Maxwell offers the best description of each. *A leader of followers needs to be needed,* he says, *and a leader of leaders wants to be exceeded.*

I chose to become a leader of leaders. Three years into building my network marketing business, I went on a spiritual retreat with my family. During the two weeks I was away from all technology, my team added over 800 new distributors. Our team was growing like crazy, and it was growing without me – not a single person had contacted me during the two weeks I was "unplugged." Why? Because I had developed *leaders* on my team.

Building a team of leaders, rather than followers, allows you to create the freedom in your life to do what you want, when you want, with who you want. Becoming a leader of leaders gives you freedom in your business and in your life.

Leadership and relationships are the cornerstone of a network marketing business that lasts. Without leadership and deep relationships, you might have some short-term success, but attrition will begin showing up in your business, and it will eventually fall apart from the bottom up.

▶ **I go deeper into the difference between being a leader of followers and a leader of leaders in my Build to Last video course. Take a look at KeithCallahan.com/BTL.**

DO

→ Leaders

Make a list of "leaders of leaders" you admire in your company, in the network marketing industry, and in general. Stretch yourself to come up with the names of 15 individuals who live (or lived) the kind of life you want to live, who model leadership qualities you admire, who you admire or envy – from your team leader to the head of your company to the coach of your high school soccer team to political figures who have changed the course of history.

1. ____________________
2. ____________________
3. ____________________
4. ____________________
5. ____________________
6. ____________________
7. ____________________
8. ____________________
9. ____________________
10. ____________________
11. ____________________
12. ____________________
13. ____________________
14. ____________________
15. ____________________

→ Thought Download on Top Leaders

Pick your top **five** from your list, and on the following pages, delve into the attributes that make each of them such inspiring, standout leaders. Do a "thought download" on each, writing down your insights and reflections on the following pages.

1. ____
2. ____
3. ____
4. ____
5. ____

▶ I go deeper into how to get into the feeling nature of being a leader in my video course – available at KeithCallahan.com/BTL.

1. Leader's name: ____________________

- What type of person are they?
- How do they make other people feel?
- What do they do differently than others?
- What skills do they possess that you admire?
- What do they do on a daily basis?
- What type of life do they live?
- What is their mindset?
- What is their leadership style?

2. Leader's name: ______________________________

- What type of person are they?
- How do they make other people feel?
- What do they do differently than others?
- What skills do they possess that you admire?
- What do they do on a daily basis?
- What type of life do they live?
- What is their mindset?
- What is their leadership style?

3. Leader's name: ____

- What type of person are they?
- How do they make other people feel?
- What do they do differently than others?
- What skills do they possess that you admire?
- What do they do on a daily basis?
- What type of life do they live?
- What is their mindset?
- What is their leadership style?

4. Leader's name: ____

- What type of person are they?
- How do they make other people feel?
- What do they do differently than others?
- What skills do they possess that you admire?
- What do they do on a daily basis?
- What type of life do they live?
- What is their mindset?
- What is their leadership style?

5. Leader's name: ____

- What type of person are they?
- How do they make other people feel?
- What do they do differently than others?
- What skills do they possess that you admire?
- What do they do on a daily basis?
- What type of life do they live?
- What is their mindset?
- What is their leadership style?

→ Your Personal, Leadership "I Am" Statement

Now, synthesize the qualities of these five leaders of leaders into a statement that begins: An ideal leader of leaders is…

Rewrite the above as an "I am" statement: I am a leader who…

Congratulations! You've just described in detail the leader of leaders that you are becoming. It's normal if this makes you uncomfortable or emotional at this stage. You're going to grow into being this leader. You are becoming this leader.

→ "I Am" Reminders

Revisit this description daily, and revise as necessary. To assist yourself in training your mind to become this leader of leaders, put reminders of your "I am" statement around your house, in your car, on your phone, in your office, and elsewhere.

ACCELERATE

Ten-minute Morning Meditation

Every morning during this module, allow yourself to really get into the *feeling nature* of the leader you're becoming. Set a timer for 10 minutes so you can relax fully, and engage all of your senses to explore in your imagination what's it going to feel like when you're being a leader yourself. The feeling of eagerness to start your day when your alarm goes off in the morning…the gratitude you feel for each of the people you had the opportunity to share this business opportunity with during the day…the café setting where you often meet with prospects…the clothes you're wearing when you get on a video-conference with your team. Allow yourself to experience yourself *today* as the leader of leaders you're becoming. That inner experience paves the way for the outer manifestation.

Daily Mantras

As you work through this module, first thing in the morning and last thing at night, repeat to yourself or aloud 10 times:

I'm looking for five leaders.

And throughout the day, allow this mantra to drive your thinking and your focus.

Ten-minute Evening Reflection

Every evening during this module, set a timer for 10 minutes of reviewing, assessing, and replaying all that went right today. Also take note of one thing that can be improved on. And most important, be in gratitude for all that went well.

At the end of this module, you'll find a habit tracker and space to record your insights and progress, one for each of seven days.

DISCUSS

Possible topics for group meetings around *Module 1, Build to Last and Leadership* – after the daily practices and action steps have been completed:

- What qualities of your top five leaders do you want to emulate?
- How do those leaders inspire people into action?
- Share your "I am" statement, and allow yourself to feel its power as the group reads back to you a description of the ideal leader of leaders that you are becoming. (They replace "I am" with "[Your name] is.")
- What doubts arise for you?
- How do you address those doubts to re-align yourself with a leader-of-leaders mindset?
- How is your new routine of meditation, mantra, and journaling affecting your day-to-day experience of becoming a leader of leaders?

A study group aims to encourage and strengthen participants (not be a pity party). If you're the facilitator of a group diving into this *Build to Last Workbook* together, make sure to model and maintain a supportive, positive tone.

TRACK

Date ____________ **Habits Check List**

- ☐ Morning meditation
- ☐ Daily mantras
- ☐ Morning mantra
- ☐ Evening reflection
- ☐ Present and follow up on product, service, and/or business opportunity
- ☐ Evening journaling
- ☐ Evening mantra

What went well?

1. ____

____

____

____

____

2. ____

____

____

____

____

3. ____

____

____

____

____

____

What could I improve? How?

Other notes

TRACK

Date ___________ **Habits Check List**

- ☐ Morning meditation
- ☐ Morning mantra
- ☐ Present and follow up on product, service, and/or business opportunity
- ☐ Daily mantras
- ☐ Evening reflection
- ☐ Evening journaling
- ☐ Evening mantra

What went well?

1. ______________________________

____

____

____

____

2. ______________________________

____

____

____

____

3. ______________________________

____

____

____

____

____

What could I improve? How?

Other notes

TRACK

Date ___________ **Habits Check List**

- ☐ Morning meditation
- ☐ Daily mantras
- ☐ Morning mantra
- ☐ Evening reflection
- ☐ Present and follow up on product, service, and/or business opportunity
- ☐ Evening journaling
- ☐ Evening mantra

What went well?

1. ____________________

____

____

____

____

2. ____________________

____

____

____

____

3. ____________________

____

____

____

____

____

What could I improve? How?

Other notes

TRACK

Date ____________ **Habits Check List**

☐ Morning meditation

☐ Morning mantra

☐ Present and follow up on product, service, and/or business opportunity

☐ Daily mantras

☐ Evening reflection

☐ Evening journaling

☐ Evening mantra

What went well?

1. ____

____

____

____

____

2. ____

____

____

____

____

3. ____

____

____

____

____

What could I improve? How?

Other notes

TRACK

Date ___________ **Habits Check List**

☐ Morning meditation

☐ Morning mantra

☐ Present and follow up on product, service, and/or business opportunity

☐ Daily mantras

☐ Evening reflection

☐ Evening journaling

☐ Evening mantra

What went well?

1. ____

____

____

____

____

2. ____

____

____

____

____

3. ____

____

____

____

____

____

What could I improve? How?

Other notes

TRACK

Date ____________ **Habits Check List**

☐ Morning meditation

☐ Daily mantras

☐ Morning mantra

☐ Evening reflection

☐ Present and follow up on product, service, and/or business opportunity

☐ Evening journaling

☐ Evening mantra

What went well?

1. ____

____

____

____

____

2. ____

____

____

____

____

3. ____

____

____

____

____

____

What could I improve? How?

Other notes

TRACK

Date ____________ **Habits Check List**

☐ Morning meditation

☐ Morning mantra

☐ Present and follow up on product, service, and/or business opportunity

☐ Daily mantras

☐ Evening reflection

☐ Evening journaling

☐ Evening mantra

What went well?

1. ____

____

____

____

____

2. ____

____

____

____

____

3. ____

____

____

____

____

____

What could I improve? How?

Other notes

Module 2
BUILD TO LAST AND LEGACY

Leadership is not about the next election,
it's about the next generation.
— Simon Sinek

GOAL

To get a clear picture of who you need to become (not what you need to do).

READ

Leaving a legacy is about making life better for those who follow you than it was for you. It's about showing people how to live better than they ever dreamed possible. Leaving a legacy starts with you, touches those you directly influence, and eventually leads to generational change.

Leaving a legacy isn't about money. Many of us make the mistake of thinking *income* is the big gift and promise of the network marketing industry. The income you can make (if you do it right) will indeed far surpass your expectations. That's not the real gift in this business, though. The real gift is being the person you have to become in order to earn the income. There are no shortcuts to the top in this industry.

You have to become a person capable of achieving success yourself before you can mentor others to success.

The blessing of this business is that the more bright, shiny, happy, content, loving, and gracious you become, the more people's lives you positively affect and the more success you see. The better version of you that you become, the more you earn.

DO

It's time to dream big and dream beautiful, creating – in your heart, in your mind, and on paper – the life you want to live. Put no limitations on what you can create, how much you can earn, how many lives you can touch, how magnificent your life can be.

This is some of the most important and foundational thought-work you will do to set yourself up to succeed. You must have a vision in order to steer yourself steadily toward it.

→ Five-year Vision

Work through this exercise in a quiet place where you won't be interrupted.

Take a couple of long, slow, deep breaths. Relax your body. Now project yourself five years into the future. What year is it? How old will you be? How old will other people in your life be? Situate yourself and start to dream bigger than you've ever allowed yourself to dream before. Imagine everything unfolding astoundingly well for you over the next five years. As a successful leader of leaders in your network marketing business, who have you become? What is your ideal self? What do your day-to-day activities look like? What is your weekly routine? How do you feel as you begin each day? What is the rhythm of your months? What are your relationships like? What type of home or homes will you have? Where? Explore in your imagination how it feels to be at home. Will you be traveling? What is your income? How do you spend your money? How does it feel? What sorts of thoughts do you have throughout the day? Who are you surrounded by? What activities do you enjoy? What is your social life like? What is NOT part of your life? Explore all aspects of your life and describe the most beautiful vision you can.

This isn't required, but if you like, do the same exercises for your 20-year and legacy visions, as well. What legacy would you be proud and gratified to leave as a gift for generations to come? Allow yourself to explore this in your heart.

→ Share Your Five-year Vision

Now synthesize these pages of writing about your five-year vision into a concise paragraph or statement that you can begin to share with others and refer to often to remind yourself of the ideal-for-you life you're in the process of creating *now*.

▶ Writing down your vision can be difficult at times. I go deeper into how to do this in my video course. Take a look at KeithCallahan.com/BTL.

ACCELERATE

Ten-minute Morning Meditation

Every morning during this module, allow yourself to really get into the *feeling nature* of living your idea life, which you have explored – or will soon explore – in the action steps detailed above. Set a timer for 10 minutes so you can relax fully, and engage all of your senses to imagine what's it going to feel like in five years, when you're leading a team of leaders and your life is exceeding the wildest dreams you could have had last year. Daydream about how your days look and feel in five years, as you've felt and described it. Imagine the "ripple effect" that you being a leader of leaders has on future generations. Allow yourself to explore and feel and enjoy the experiences of your ideal life. That inner experience paves the way for the outer manifestation.

Daily Mantras

As you work through this module, first thing in the morning and last thing at night, repeat to yourself or aloud 10 times:

I have the ability to help people change their lives.

And throughout the day, allow this mantra to drive your thinking and your focus.

Ten-minute Evening Reflection

Every evening during this module, set a timer for 10 minutes and begin to establish a practice of reviewing, assessing, and replaying all that went right today. Also take note of one thing that can be improved on. And most important, be in gratitude for all that went well.

At the end of this module, you'll find a habit tracker and space to record your insights and progress, one for each of seven days.

DISCUSS

Possible topics for group meetings around *Module 2, Build to Last and Legacy* – after the daily practices and action steps have been completed:

- What is the high level of your big, beautiful dream?
- Share some of the business specifics of your five-year vision?
- Share some of the personal details of your five -year vision?
- What evidence do you have from your own life that the "better" version of yourself you are, the more successful you are in your business?

▶ While dreaming your dreams is important, one of the ways to accelerate your business further is to help your TEAM dream too. I go deeper into how to unlock your team's dreams in the Build to Last video course available at KeithCallahan.com/BTL.

TRACK

Date ____________ **Habits Check List**

☐ Morning meditation

☐ Morning mantra

☐ Present and follow up on product, service, and/or business opportunity

☐ Daily mantras

☐ Evening reflection

☐ Evening journaling

☐ Evening mantra

What went well?

1. ____

____

____

____

____

2. ____

____

____

____

____

3. ____

____

____

____

____

What could I improve? How?

Other notes

TRACK

Date ____________ **Habits Check List**

☐ Morning meditation

☐ Morning mantra

☐ Present and follow up on product, service, and/or business opportunity

☐ Daily mantras

☐ Evening reflection

☐ Evening journaling

☐ Evening mantra

What went well?

1. ____

____

____

____

____

2. ____

____

____

____

____

3. ____

____

____

____

____

____

What could I improve? How?

Other notes

TRACK

Date ____________ **Habits Check List**

☐ Morning meditation

☐ Morning mantra

☐ Present and follow up on product, service, and/or business opportunity

☐ Daily mantras

☐ Evening reflection

☐ Evening journaling

☐ Evening mantra

What went well?

1. ____

____

____

____

____

2. ____

____

____

____

____

3. ____

____

____

____

____

____

What could I improve? How?

Other notes

TRACK

Date ____________ **Habits Check List**

☐ Morning meditation

☐ Morning mantra

☐ Present and follow up on product, service, and/or business opportunity

☐ Daily mantras

☐ Evening reflection

☐ Evening journaling

☐ Evening mantra

What went well?

1. ____

____

____

____

____

2. ____

____

____

____

____

3. ____

____

____

____

____

____

What could I improve? How?

Other notes

TRACK

Date ____________ **Habits Check List**

☐ Morning meditation

☐ Morning mantra

☐ Present and follow up on product, service, and/or business opportunity

☐ Daily mantras

☐ Evening reflection

☐ Evening journaling

☐ Evening mantra

What went well?

1. ____

____

____

____

____

2. ____

____

____

____

____

3. ____

____

____

____

____

____

What could I improve? How?

Other notes

TRACK

Date ____________ **Habits Check List**

☐ Morning meditation

☐ Morning mantra

☐ Present and follow up on product, service, and/or business opportunity

☐ Daily mantras

☐ Evening reflection

☐ Evening journaling

☐ Evening mantra

What went well?

1. ____

____

____

____

____

2. ____

____

____

____

____

3. ____

____

____

____

____

____

What could I improve? How?

Other notes

TRACK

Date ___________ **Habits Check List**

☐ Morning meditation

☐ Morning mantra

☐ Present and follow up on product, service, and/or business opportunity

☐ Daily mantras

☐ Evening reflection

☐ Evening journaling

☐ Evening mantra

What went well?

1. ______________________________

____

____

____

____

2. ______________________________

____

____

____

____

3. ______________________________

____

____

____

____

____

What could I improve? How?

Other notes

Module 3

THE BUILD-TO-LAST MINDSET

Leadership is practiced not so much in words as in attitude and in actions.
— Harold S. Geneen

GOAL

To live, sleep, and breathe the seven philosophies for leading yourself, so you can embody them in your day-to-day activities.

READ

A leader's philosophy on life and how to build a network marketing business is significantly different from that of distributors who are *not* leaders. In order to start leading others, you must first lead yourself. Following are seven core philosophies for leading yourself.

1. Leaders focus on who they are becoming more than what they are getting.

A leader's mindset is not about activities, rewards, or accolades. Leading is about changing yourself from the inside out.

2. Leaders don't just believe they can, they know they will.

There is a vital difference between believing you can do something and knowing without a doubt that you will do it. This *knowing* piece is the internal shift many would-be leaders never make. Until you do, people won't be attracted to you or want to join you.

3. Leaders don't just "show up," they show up with their mind right.

Leaders know that just plowing along when their mind isn't right does not lead to success in this business. The actions – the corporate trainings, sharing products and business opportunities, following up – that is five percent of success. Ninety-five percent of enduring success is the mindset, the thoughts, the feelings *behind* the actions you're taking.

4. Leaders understand they own a "big business."

Leaders in our industry don't look at their network marketing business as a little side gig to make some extra money here and there. When I first got started, I played a mind trick on myself. Despite the low start-up cost and the opportunity being open to anyone, I asked myself, "How seriously would I take this business if the cost of failing was $250,000?" That thought added a level of urgency, of motivation to the way I approached this business.

5. Leaders set one overarching, long-term goal.
Look at your business and decide what you want it to do for you. What single, long-term goal will help you get the most out of your business? Not the goal that corporate wants you to hit, but the goal that is going to give you the life you want. After your goal is set, make sure all your daily activities are in line with that goal.

6. Leaders create momentum and ride it.
Building momentum and riding it like a wave is much less work than crashing around in the surf of your fears, insecurities, self-doubt, lack of success and skills when you're first getting started. As we move through these pieces one by one and start to see some small wins, we get closer to the wave. Riding the momentum promotes massive growth in your business and is fun.

7. Leaders give themselves permission to succeed.
So many of us are waiting for permission to become the person we're capable of becoming in this business. Right now, as you're reading, I want you to hear and I want you to feel – from my heart to yours – that you have permission to succeed at the highest levels in this business.

▶ In the Build to Last video course, I go deeper into how a leader thinks and acts on a daily basis. You can learn more at KeithCallahan.com/BTL.

DO

Set aside a few hours to hone in on what you are working toward in your business. Work through the following exercises in a quiet place where you won't be interrupted.

→ Five-year Financial Goal

Referring to the action steps from the last module, bring back to mind the life you want to be living five years from now. It's time to specify the long-term five-year income goal you will work toward to support that life. Don't get hung up trying to be too precise, but do get into some detail as you work to identify a meaningful, compelling number that stretches your imagination. Consider all the monthly expenses of the life you're growing into, what you want to be saving, what you want to invest, your budget for travel or philanthropy, etc., and write this declaration below: I earn $_______ in the year ____.

____

Congratulations! That's a powerful step!

Keep that financial goal at the center of all your daily activities. During your working hours, check in with yourself often to make sure you focus only on activities that support your goal.

→ Three- to Six-month Financial Goal

Decide on a three- to six-month financial goal that is a stepping stone for your five-year goal. Write it below, and make it your "push" goal over the next three to six months: My push goal for the next ____ months is $______.

____

Get in the habit of checking in with yourself and your numbers at the end of each week. Are you moving toward your push goal?

→ "I Am" Statements

To keep you in the mindset of your short-term and long-term goals, come up with "I am" statements around the concept of giving yourself permission to succeed at the highest levels in your business. As we've noted, an "I am" statement is simply a powerful, positive affirmation starting with "I am" that creates within you feelings of motivation, focus, discipline, enthusiasm, purposefulness, and the like.

Write 10-20 statements to roll around in your mind throughout the day. Examples:

- I am becoming a leader of leaders.
- I am empowered.
- I am confident.
- I am clear about my goals.
- I am in the process of achieving my goals.
- I am creating the success I've dreamed of.

1. ______________________________
2. ______________________________
3. ______________________________
4. ______________________________
5. ______________________________
6. ______________________________
7. ______________________________
8. ______________________________
9. ______________________________

10. ______________________________
11. ______________________________
12. ______________________________
13. ______________________________
14. ______________________________
15. ______________________________
16. ______________________________
17. ______________________________
18. ______________________________
19. ______________________________
20. ______________________________

ACCELERATE

Ten-minute Morning Meditation

Every morning during this module, allow yourself to really get into the *feeling nature* of one of the core philosophies of self-leaders. Set a timer for 10 minutes so you can relax fully and have an inner experience of the philosophy you're focusing on for the day.

1. Leaders focus on who they are becoming more than what they are getting.
2. Leaders don't just believe they can, they know they will.
3. Leaders don't just "show up," they show up with their mind right.
4. Leaders understand they own a "big business."
5. Leaders set one overarching, long-term goal.
6. Leaders create momentum and ride it.
7. Leaders give themselves permission to succeed.

Daily Mantras

As you work through this module, first thing in the morning and last thing at night, repeat to yourself or aloud 10 times the philosophy you chose to meditate on. And 100 times throughout the day, allow this mantra to drive your thinking, your focus, and your actions.

Ten-minute Evening Reflection

Every evening during this module, set a timer for 10 minutes of reviewing, assessing, and replaying all that went right today. Also take note of one thing that can be improved on. And most important, be in gratitude for all that went well.

At the end of this module, you'll find a habit tracker and space to record your insights and progress, one for each of seven days.

DISCUSS

For group meetings around *Module 3, The Build-to-last Mindset* – after the daily practices and action steps have been completed – consider inviting people to share their experiences with each of the seven core philosophies of self-leadership:

- Resistance to
- Doubts that arise
- Day-to-day embodiment of
- Successes related to

The seven core philosophies:

1. Leaders focus on who they are becoming more than what they are getting.
2. Leaders don't just believe they can, they know they will.
3. Leaders don't just "show up," they show up with their mind right.
4. Leaders understand they own a "big business."
5. Leaders set one overarching, long-term goal.
6. Leaders create momentum and ride it.
7. Leaders give themselves permission to succeed.

TRACK

Date ___________ **Habits Check List**

☐ Morning meditation

☐ Daily mantras

☐ Morning mantra

☐ Evening reflection

☐ Present and follow up on product, service, and/or business opportunity

☐ Evening journaling

☐ Evening mantra

What went well?

1. ____

____

____

____

____

2. ____

____

____

____

3. ____

____

____

____

____

What could I improve? How?

Other notes

TRACK

Date ____________

Habits Check List

☐ Morning meditation

☐ Morning mantra

☐ Present and follow up on product, service, and/or business opportunity

☐ Daily mantras

☐ Evening reflection

☐ Evening journaling

☐ Evening mantra

What went well?

1. ____

____

____

____

____

2. ____

____

____

____

____

3. ____

____

____

____

____

____

What could I improve? How?

Other notes

TRACK

Date ____________ **Habits Check List**

☐ Morning meditation

☐ Daily mantras

☐ Morning mantra

☐ Evening reflection

☐ Present and follow up on product, service, and/or business opportunity

☐ Evening journaling

☐ Evening mantra

What went well?

1. ____________________

2. ____________________

3. ____________________

What could I improve? How?

Other notes

TRACK

Date ____________ **Habits Check List**

☐ Morning meditation

☐ Morning mantra

☐ Present and follow up on product, service, and/or business opportunity

☐ Daily mantras

☐ Evening reflection

☐ Evening journaling

☐ Evening mantra

What went well?

1. ______________________________

____

____

____

____

2. ______________________________

____

____

____

____

3. ______________________________

____

____

____

____

____

What could I improve? How?

Other notes

TRACK

Date ___________ **Habits Check List**

☐ Morning meditation

☐ Morning mantra

☐ Present and follow up on product, service, and/or business opportunity

☐ Daily mantras

☐ Evening reflection

☐ Evening journaling

☐ Evening mantra

What went well?

1. ____

____

____

____

____

2. ____

____

____

____

____

3. ____

____

____

____

____

____

What could I improve? How?

Other notes

TRACK

Date ___________ **Habits Check List**

☐ Morning meditation

☐ Daily mantras

☐ Morning mantra

☐ Evening reflection

☐ Present and follow up on product, service, and/or business opportunity

☐ Evening journaling

☐ Evening mantra

What went well?

1. ______________________________

____

____

____

____

2. ______________________________

____

____

____

____

3. ______________________________

____

____

____

____

____

What could I improve? How?

Other notes

TRACK

Date ____________ **Habits Check List**

- ☐ Morning meditation
- ☐ Daily mantras
- ☐ Morning mantra
- ☐ Evening reflection
- ☐ Present and follow up on product, service, and/or business opportunity
- ☐ Evening journaling
- ☐ Evening mantra

What went well?

1. ______________________________

____

____

____

____

2. ______________________________

____

____

____

____

3. ______________________________

____

____

____

____

____

What could I improve? How?

Other notes

Module 4

BUILD TO LAST AND YOUR PERSONAL DEVELOPMENT PLAN

As a leader, it's a major responsibility on your shoulders to practice the behavior you want others to follow.

— Himanshu Bhatia

GOAL

To map out and begin implementing your unique personal development plan.

READ

Most of us have a major misconception about personal development. We think personal development is something you just sit down and do. Read 10 pages a day. Listen to the podcast on your ride to work. Jump on the training call. This, however, is just information gathering, which is useless if we don't do anything with it.

Personal development – the process of *developing* yourself as a *person* – involves understanding "who you are" right now and "who you need to be" in order to achieve your goals and dreams.

Most distributors fall short by focusing on "what are the activities that I have to do?" *Leaders* focus on "who is the person I need to become in order to build the team I want?" Once you get clear on who you are and who you need to be, you can then look for the resources to close the gap.

And here is the important part: you need to do more than study and learn, you need to *implement*. You need to *become!*

PS While you're working on your personal development plan, make sure you're also working on your business. We're in a "do and then learn business." So get out there. It's okay to be uncomfortable. Take the action. That's the way you learn how to do it a little better next time.

▶ PPS I'm very passionate about personal development, which I delve into deeply in the Build to Last video course. I'll teach you what REAL personal development is, and how you can attract the success you desire by becoming the person you need and want to become. Go to KeithCallahan.com/BTL.

DO

In this module, we'll put together your personal development plan as it relates to your network marketing business.

→ Leaders

Start by jotting down 10 leaders in your company and other leaders you admire (check your list from Module 1).

1. ______________________________
2. ______________________________
3. ______________________________
4. ______________________________
5. ______________________________
6. ______________________________
7. ______________________________
8. ______________________________
9. ______________________________
10. ______________________________

→ Qualities of Leaders

Below, list qualities you admire in those leaders – from technical leadership skills to self-esteem to how they make others feel. You may admire somebody for her ability to inspire others. You may admire another person for the duplicatable systems he created for his team. You may admire yet another leader for the way he always brings in top-quality people or for his trustworthy character. Consider how those leaders inspire their team and how those leaders make the individuals on their team feel.

Inventory of leaders' qualities:

1. ______________________________
2. ______________________________
3. ______________________________
4. ______________________________
5. ______________________________
6. ______________________________
7. ______________________________
8. ______________________________
9. ______________________________
10. ______________________________

You've just defined your idea of the pinnacle qualities of leadership, in other words, *your ideal self* as a leader in network marketing on a more granular level than we got to in Module 1.

→ Personal Qualities Inventory

It's time to take an honest gut check: where are you right now? Below, rate yourself on a scale of 1 to 10 for each of the qualities you're looking to grow into. You take the inventory so you can see the gap. Once you see the gap, you know where you need to improve.

Reflect on how you would feel and how you would act if you were a 10 in each of these areas, and make some notes for yourself.

1. Quality ______________________________

Current level from 1 to 10: ________

How I would feel and act:

____

____

____

____

____

____

____

____

2. Quality ______________________________

Current level from 1 to 10: ________

How I would feel and act:

____

____

____

____

____

____

____

____

3. Quality ______________________________

Current level from 1 to 10: __________

How I would feel and act:

____

____

____

____

____

____

____

____

4. Quality ______________________________

Current level from 1 to 10: __________

How I would feel and act:

____

____

____

____

____

____

____

____

5. Quality ____

Current level from 1 to 10: ___________

How I would feel and act:

____

____

____

____

____

____

____

____

6. Quality ____

Current level from 1 to 10: ___________

How I would feel and act:

____

____

____

____

____

____

____

____

7. Quality ______________________________

Current level from 1 to 10: ________

How I would feel and act:

____

____

____

____

____

____

____

____

8. Quality ______________________________

Current level from 1 to 10: ________

How I would feel and act:

____

____

____

____

____

____

____

____

9. Quality ____

Current level from 1 to 10: ___________

How I would feel and act:

____

____

____

____

____

____

____

____

10. Quality ____

Current level from 1 to 10: ___________

How I would feel and act:

____

____

____

____

____

____

____

____

Now you have a clear understanding of where you are today and where you want to be. Your improvement plan covers the distance between the two.

▶ If you need further clarity on how to become the leader you want to be, check out my video course at KeithCallahan.com/BTL.

→ Focus Qualities

Given your list of qualities and your current rating, reflect on the long-term and short-term goals you put together in Module 3. With those goals in mind, what three qualities, if improved, will have the biggest positive impact on the achievement of your goals?

1. Quality ________________________________

2. Quality ________________________________

3. Quality ________________________________

→ Act and Track

Reread your description of yourself at a 10 in each of these three improvement areas, and take immediate action today. Keep it simple. Just take the first step – it could be making a phone call, making a list, setting an appointment, buying a book.

Continue to take daily action in the same manner, and monitor your progress in the TRACK section.

- Are you closing the gaps?
- What's working?
- What's not working?
- What is your strategy to address what's not working?

ACCELERATE

Ten-minute Morning Meditation

Every morning during this module, allow yourself to really get into the *feeling nature* of yourself being a 10 regarding one of the three qualities you identified as having the biggest positive impact on the achievement of your goals. Set a timer for 10 minutes so you can relax fully, and engage all of your senses to explore in your imagination who you are *being* and what looks and feels like. That inner experience paves the way for the outer manifestation.

Daily Mantras

As you work through this module, first thing in the morning and last thing at night, repeat to yourself or aloud 10 times a mantra related to the quality or qualities you're focusing on. For example:

I am a leader of leaders known for taking massive action.

Repeat this mantra 100 times throughout the day, allow it to drive your thinking and your focus.

Ten-minute Evening Reflection

Every evening during this module, set a timer for 10 minutes of reviewing, assessing, and replaying all that went right today. Also take note of one thing that can be improved on. And most important, be in gratitude for all that went well.

At the end of this module, you'll find a habit tracker and space to record your insights and progress, one for each of seven days.

DISCUSS

Possible topics for group meetings around *Module 4, Build to Last and Your Personal Development Plan* – after the daily practices and action steps have been completed:

- What insights arose as you created your personal development plan?
- What qualities of an ideal leader did you identify?
- What three qualities are you focusing on?
- What accelerator practices are the most effective for you?
- Have you noticed a difference in the way people respond to you over the course of these four modules?

TRACK

Date ___________ **Habits Check List**

☐ Morning meditation

☐ Morning mantra

☐ Present and follow up on product, service, and/or business opportunity

☐ Daily mantras

☐ Evening reflection

☐ Evening journaling

☐ Evening mantra

What went well?

1. ____

____

____

____

____

2. ____

____

____

____

____

3. ____

____

____

____

____

____

What could I improve? How?

Other notes

TRACK

Date ___________ **Habits Check List**

☐ Morning meditation

☐ Morning mantra

☐ Present and follow up on product, service, and/or business opportunity

☐ Daily mantras

☐ Evening reflection

☐ Evening journaling

☐ Evening mantra

What went well?

1. ____

____

____

____

____

2. ____

____

____

____

____

3. ____

____

____

____

____

____

What could I improve? How?

Other notes

TRACK

Date ____________ **Habits Check List**

☐ Morning meditation

☐ Morning mantra

☐ Present and follow up on product, service, and/or business opportunity

☐ Daily mantras

☐ Evening reflection

☐ Evening journaling

☐ Evening mantra

What went well?

1. ____

____

____

____

____

2. ____

____

____

____

____

3. ____

____

____

____

____

____

What could I improve? How?

Other notes

TRACK

Date ____________ **Habits Check List**

☐ Morning meditation

☐ Morning mantra

☐ Present and follow up on product, service, and/or business opportunity

☐ Daily mantras

☐ Evening reflection

☐ Evening journaling

☐ Evening mantra

What went well?

1. ____

____

____

____

____

2. ____

____

____

____

____

3. ____

____

____

____

____

____

What could I improve? How?

Other notes

TRACK

Date ____________ **Habits Check List**

☐ Morning meditation

☐ Morning mantra

☐ Present and follow up on product, service, and/or business opportunity

☐ Daily mantras

☐ Evening reflection

☐ Evening journaling

☐ Evening mantra

What went well?

1. ____

____

____

____

____

2. ____

____

____

____

____

3. ____

____

____

____

____

What could I improve? How?

Other notes

TRACK

Date ____________ **Habits Check List**

☐ Morning meditation

☐ Daily mantras

☐ Morning mantra

☐ Evening reflection

☐ Present and follow up on product, service, and/or business opportunity

☐ Evening journaling

☐ Evening mantra

What went well?

1. ____

____

____

____

____

2. ____

____

____

____

____

3. ____

____

____

____

____

____

What could I improve? How?

Other notes

TRACK

Date ____________ **Habits Check List**

- ☐ Morning meditation
- ☐ Daily mantras
- ☐ Morning mantra
- ☐ Evening reflection
- ☐ Present and follow up on product, service, and/or business opportunity
- ☐ Evening journaling
- ☐ Evening mantra

What went well?

1. ____

____

____

____

____

2. ____

____

____

____

____

3. ____

____

____

____

____

____

What could I improve? How?

Other notes

Module 5

BUILD TO LAST AND YOUR BELIEF

A genuine leader is not a searcher
for consensus but a molder of consensus.
— Martin Luther King, Jr.

GOAL

To share your opportunity from your deep belief in the gift of network marketing.

READ

For new distributors and even seasoned distributors, one of the biggest obstacles to building a large organization is not recognizing the value of what you have to offer. People are looking for an opportunity, but most distributors are caught up in worrying about what others think and miss the chance to serve. We can be hesitant to approach friends, acquaintances, and strangers for fear of bothering them. We don't want to continue to follow up for fear of pestering or pressuring. We feel like we're always trying to push our business opportunity or products on other people. Have you ever felt that way? Do you feel that way right now?

It's a block to building a large organization. Heck, it's a block to getting your business off the ground. So take the step of recognizing and embracing the value of the opportunity of network marketing.

The network marketing industry has the ability to save lives. Don't think otherwise.

People living paycheck to paycheck, getting their car repossessed, defaulting on their mortgage, people who aren't connecting with their family because they're exhausted and don't have the time – they need a way out of the pressure. In situations like these, network marketing can offer the ability to take back your life. That's the opportunity we offer. That's what this business is about. It happened for me. It has happened for so many people I've mentored. And it has been happening for over 100 years in our industry.

▶ It can be hard to communicate just what a gift that we have to offer prospective distributors. I go into this more in the *Build to Last* video course. Go to KeithCallahan.com/BTL.

DO

People in our industry get nervous about approaching others for fear of being perceived as pushy or invasive. Actually this isn't about YOU. It's about the enormous potential of the opportunity you offer and the person you're sharing it with.

→ Connecting with Struggle and Opportunity

The biggest obstacle to your success is your own limiting beliefs. Now is the time to let them go. To do this, first reread the story "A Helping Hand Can Save Someone," starting on page 68 of *Build to Last*.

With that story in mind, reflect on and write about some of the many things that people you know and encounter are struggling with:

____

____

____

____

____

____

____

____

____

____

____

____

____

Now reflect on and write about the life-changing benefits of the opportunity, all the things this opportunity can help them with:

Your goal is to share your opportunity from a deep belief in the gift of network marketing, which means releasing the thought that what you offer is burdensome in any way.

ACCELERATE

Ten-minute Morning Meditation

As you work through this module, before your morning meditation, read to yourself or declare aloud: *What I have to offer is a gift, not a burden. I've made the decision to let go of any fear of approaching others with my opportunity. I know our industry has the ability to change the lives of those who join and the generations who follow.*

Allow yourself to really get into the *feeling nature* of acting from this belief. Set a timer for 10 minutes so you can relax fully, and engage all of your senses to explore in your imagination how you move through the day, interacting with people, sharing the gift of your opportunity. That inner experience paves the way for the outer manifestation.

Daily Mantras

As you work through this module, first thing in the morning and last thing at night, repeat to yourself or aloud 10 times:

I approach others with an opportunity
that can help them realize their biggest dreams.

And 100 times throughout the day, allow this mantra to drive your thinking and your focus.

Ten-minute Evening Reflection

Every evening during this module, set a timer for 10 minutes of reviewing, assessing, and replaying all that went right today. Also take note of one thing that can be improved on. And most important, be in gratitude for all that went well.

At the end of this module, you'll find a habit tracker and space to record your insights and progress, one for each of seven days.

DISCUSS

Possible topics for group meetings around *Module 5, Build to Last and Your Belief*—after the daily practices and action steps have been completed:

- On a scale of 1 to 10, rate your belief in the opportunity of network marketing as a gift that can change the lives of people you encounter both BEFORE you worked through this module and AFTER.
- How is your deep belief affecting the way you interact with prospective distributors and the way they respond to you?
- What stories of transformation do you share with prospective distributors?

▶ I help you deepen your belief that it's not about you in the *Build to Last* video course. You can take a look at KeithCallahan.com/BTL.

TRACK

Date ___________ **Habits Check List**

☐ Morning meditation

☐ Morning mantra

☐ Present and follow up on product, service, and/or business opportunity

☐ Daily mantras

☐ Evening reflection

☐ Evening journaling

☐ Evening mantra

What went well?

1. ____

____

____

____

____

2. ____

____

____

____

____

3. ____

____

____

____

____

____

What could I improve? How?

Other notes

TRACK

Date ___________ **Habits Check List**

- ☐ Morning meditation
- ☐ Daily mantras
- ☐ Morning mantra
- ☐ Evening reflection
- ☐ Present and follow up on product, service, and/or business opportunity
- ☐ Evening journaling
- ☐ Evening mantra

What went well?

1. ____

2. ____

3. ____

What could I improve? How?

Other notes

TRACK

Date ___________ **Habits Check List**

☐ Morning meditation

☐ Daily mantras

☐ Morning mantra

☐ Evening reflection

☐ Present and follow up on product, service, and/or business opportunity

☐ Evening journaling

☐ Evening mantra

What went well?

1. ____

____

____

____

____

2. ____

____

____

____

____

3. ____

____

____

____

____

____

What could I improve? How?

Other notes

TRACK

Date ____________ **Habits Check List**

☐ Morning meditation

☐ Morning mantra

☐ Present and follow up on product, service, and/or business opportunity

☐ Daily mantras

☐ Evening reflection

☐ Evening journaling

☐ Evening mantra

What went well?

1. ______________________________

____

____

____

____

2. ______________________________

____

____

____

____

3. ______________________________

____

____

____

____

____

What could I improve? How?

Other notes

TRACK

Date ___________ **Habits Check List**

☐ Morning meditation

☐ Morning mantra

☐ Present and follow up on product, service, and/or business opportunity

☐ Daily mantras

☐ Evening reflection

☐ Evening journaling

☐ Evening mantra

What went well?

1. ____

____

____

____

____

2. ____

____

____

____

____

3. ____

____

____

____

____

____

What could I improve? How?

Other notes

TRACK

Date ___________ **Habits Check List**

☐ Morning meditation

☐ Morning mantra

☐ Present and follow up on product, service, and/or business opportunity

☐ Daily mantras

☐ Evening reflection

☐ Evening journaling

☐ Evening mantra

What went well?

1. ______________________________

2. ______________________________

3. ______________________________

What could I improve? How?

Other notes

TRACK

Date ___________ **Habits Check List**

☐ Morning meditation

☐ Morning mantra

☐ Present and follow up on product, service, and/or business opportunity

☐ Daily mantras

☐ Evening reflection

☐ Evening journaling

☐ Evening mantra

What went well?

1. ____

____

____

____

____

2. ____

____

____

____

____

3. ____

____

____

____

____

____

What could I improve? How?

Other notes

Module 6

POSITIONING YOURSELF AS A LEADER

I am not afraid of an army of lions led by a sheep;
I am afraid of an army of sheep led by a lion.
— Alexander the Great

GOAL

To convey to everyone you come across in this business that you know what you're doing and where you're going, and you can lead them to success too.

READ

To build a team of leaders, you must position yourself as a leader from your initial contact. How do you do this?

Approach your business with faith, enthusiasm, and action.

- **Faith** in yourself and your business. Faith in the ability of network marketing to work for you. Faith that you can build this with or without any potential distributor.
- **Enthusiasm** is like a magic wand. When you know where you're going, when people can feel your energy and enthusiasm about your opportunity, they become enthusiastic alongside you.
- **Action** is simply doing the work every single day, putting in the hours, week after week, month after month, year after year.

Present a once-in-a-lifetime opportunity.
Whether one-on-one, on social media, or wherever else you talk about your business, your emphasis is always about your next new, big thing. This special situation is coming up, and you're looking for partners to join you – for example, a new training, a new face to the company, a new product release, a new territory.

Position yourself as the one in charge, as the leader.
When someone is interested in signing up with you, these four tools to position you as the one in charge:

1. *An application.* Regardless of how a person comes to you, the application is part of the positioning process. Don't skip it because you want to rush to sign people up.
2. *A follow-up phone or video interview.* My willingness to spend half an hour with somebody who hasn't signed up yet gives me leverage because many other distributors are not willing to get on the phone with a prospect. Doing so says a lot. It also starts our relationship-building process.
3. *A welcome email with a checklist and a questionnaire.* The checklist sets up new people to succeed by taking action right away. It also gives me the

opportunity to stress what I think is important, not what corporate thinks is important. Corporate is not focused on building leaders, therefore, their welcome email is likely to be very different from my welcome email.

4. *A "getting started right" call.* When I start new distributors, they're usually signing up people within the first day. The first week at the longest.

The entire getting-started process indicates to new distributors that they're going to work and it's going to be uncomfortable, but you are going to set goals and show them exactly what to do right from the start. So when distributors sign up with you, they may be nervous – just like all new distributors – but they take action right away.

▶ Positioning yourself as a leader is REALLY important. I go into this in more detail in the *Build to Last* video course. Take a look at KeithCallahan.com/BTL.

DO

Your long-term goal is building leaders in your downline. This starts with building relationships with distributors who recognize you as a leader from the start.

→ Professional Communications

Commit to your own professionalism, and download my templates and audio files at ***KeithCallahan.com/book*** to use in creating your own scripts and documents:

1. The question-by-question application I use to position myself as a leader.
2. The exact auto-responder I use to get potential distributors texting me to set up a call after they fill out the application.
3. The flow of my interview and a checklist for the steps to take during your interview call.
4. An audio file explaining exactly what I'm doing and what I say during the interview call to position myself as a leader.
5. The welcome email I send to new distributors and the specific 10 tasks I have them do before they get started (again, positioning me as a leader).

Add your logo, change the questions so they're customized to your situation, and the like, to personalize each of these documents to fit your business and the opportunities YOU see in the business you're building. Have someone proofread the written documents so they're clear, compelling, and free of typos.

→ Review Your Communications

Go through the last few weeks of recruiting content that you've put on social media. When you review that, ask yourself if you're positioning yourself as a leader in this industry, someone who people would follow, someone who's inspiring?

If not, list things you can do to change that.

1. ______________________________
2. ______________________________
3. ______________________________
4. ______________________________
5. ______________________________

→ Ongoing

- Continue to read and embody your "I am" statement from Module 1 – being, as fully as possible, the ideal leader you're becoming.
- Continue to work your personal development plan.

▶ EXTRA TRAINING OPPORTUNITY: Dive deeper into answering the two questions that go through every prospect's mind (they'll never ask you though). Access the training at KeithCallahan.com/BTL.

ACCELERATE

Ten-minute Morning Meditation

Every morning during this module, allow yourself to really get into the *feeling nature* of being the one in charge, of seeing yourself as a leader, of knowing you would love to work with a particular person as a distributor, but you don't *need* them. You have something to offer that *they* need. Leading others begins with being a leader from the first interaction.

Set a timer for 10 minutes so you can relax fully, and engage all of your senses to explore being a leader – from the first interaction through the "getting started right" call – in your imagination. That inner experience paves the way for the outer manifestation.

Daily Mantras

As you work through this module, first thing in the morning and last thing at night, repeat to yourself or aloud 10 times:

I position myself as a leader with each new opportunity to share my business.

And 100 times throughout the day, allow this mantra to drive your thinking and your focus.

Ten-minute Evening Reflection

Every evening during this module, set a timer for 10 minutes of reviewing, assessing, and replaying all that went right today. Also take note of one thing that can be improved on. And most important, be in gratitude for all that went well.

At the end of this module, you'll find a habit tracker and space to record your insights and progress, one for each of seven days.

DISCUSS

Possible topics for group meetings around *Module 6, Positioning Yourself as a Leader* – after the daily practices and action steps have been completed:

- How are you doing with the process of positioning yourself as the one in change with an application, interview, welcome email, and "getting started right" call?
- How are you conveying to people from the first contact that you would love to work with them but you don't need them?
- Are you using the ACCELERATE practices, and are they serving you? In what ways?

TRACK

Date ___________ **Habits Check List**

☐ Morning meditation

☐ Daily mantras

☐ Morning mantra

☐ Evening reflection

☐ Present and follow up on product, service, and/or business opportunity

☐ Evening journaling

☐ Evening mantra

What went well?

1. ____

____

____

____

____

2. ____

____

____

____

____

3. ____

____

____

____

____

____

What could I improve? How?

Other notes

TRACK

Date ____________ **Habits Check List**

- ☐ Morning meditation
- ☐ Daily mantras
- ☐ Morning mantra
- ☐ Evening reflection
- ☐ Present and follow up on product, service, and/or business opportunity
- ☐ Evening journaling
- ☐ Evening mantra

What went well?

1. ______________________________

____

____

____

____

2. ______________________________

____

____

____

____

3. ______________________________

____

____

____

____

____

What could I improve? How?

Other notes

TRACK

Date ____________

Habits Check List

- ☐ Morning meditation
- ☐ Morning mantra
- ☐ Present and follow up on product, service, and/or business opportunity
- ☐ Daily mantras
- ☐ Evening reflection
- ☐ Evening journaling
- ☐ Evening mantra

What went well?

1. ____

____

____

____

____

2. ____

____

____

____

____

3. ____

____

____

____

____

____

What could I improve? How?

Other notes

TRACK

Date ____________ **Habits Check List**

- ☐ Morning meditation
- ☐ Daily mantras
- ☐ Morning mantra
- ☐ Evening reflection
- ☐ Present and follow up on product, service, and/or business opportunity
- ☐ Evening journaling
- ☐ Evening mantra

What went well?

1. ____

____

____

____

____

2. ____

____

____

____

____

3. ____

____

____

____

____

____

What could I improve? How?

Other notes

TRACK

Date ____________ **Habits Check List**

☐ Morning meditation

☐ Daily mantras

☐ Morning mantra

☐ Evening reflection

☐ Present and follow up on product, service, and/or business opportunity

☐ Evening journaling

☐ Evening mantra

What went well?

1. ____

____

____

____

____

2. ____

____

____

____

____

3. ____

____

____

____

____

____

What could I improve? How?

Other notes

TRACK

Date ___________ **Habits Check List**

- ☐ Morning meditation
- ☐ Morning mantra
- ☐ Present and follow up on product, service, and/or business opportunity
- ☐ Daily mantras
- ☐ Evening reflection
- ☐ Evening journaling
- ☐ Evening mantra

What went well?

1. ____

____

____

____

____

2. ____

____

____

____

____

3. ____

____

____

____

____

____

What could I improve? How?

Other notes

TRACK

Date ____________ **Habits Check List**

- ☐ Morning meditation
- ☐ Morning mantra
- ☐ Present and follow up on product, service, and/or business opportunity
- ☐ Daily mantras
- ☐ Evening reflection
- ☐ Evening journaling
- ☐ Evening mantra

What went well?

1. ____

____

____

____

____

2. ____

____

____

____

____

3. ____

____

____

____

____

____

What could I improve? How?

Other notes

Module 7
ATTRACTING LEADERS

Leadership is the ability to guide others without force into a direction or decision that leaves them still feeling empowered and accomplished.

— Lisa Cash Hanson

GOAL

To commit to "getting the boulder over the hill" by orienting your mindset and your life around temporary, massive imbalance.

READ

Attracting leaders is 100 percent about your energy, your story, your vision, your dream. It's not about your products, services, or business opportunity. Think about it like you're a magnet looking to attract that perfect prospect. The more magnetic you are, the more people are drawn to you. People are attracted to you, follow you, and eventually become a partner of yours because they're inspired by who you are and what you stand for.

Success at the highest levels in our industry requires attracting leaders to partner with. Attracting leaders requires enormous energy. You have to "get the boulder over the hill" – that is, you have to get your business to the point that it starts to run away from you. When you attract other leaders and they start building their businesses, eventually your business thrives with or without you. Getting the boulder over the hill is when your team is producing exponentially more than you personally are producing. But *you* have to get that boulder over the hill, which takes massive imbalance and energy in the beginning.

Results don't come overnight. You have to see it and believe it and know it before it actually happens. And you have to have patience. Then, it's about talking to more and more people, and staying in action.

Get that boulder over the hill until you have so many leaders in your business, so many new distributors coming in every month, that it doesn't matter what YOU do.

Your leaders and team are going to have a much larger impact than you because of the foundation you laid. That's where you're going. Be prepared for it to take roughly six months before you start seeing the results.

DO

This chapter's action step is a big one: commit to one year of imbalance.

Are you willing to make this commitment to the massive action required of "getting the boulder over the hill"?

→Your Five-year Vision

Revisit the five-year vision you mapped out in Module 2. Is it worth a year of imbalance to make those dreams your reality?

→ What Can Go?

Assuming you are willing to lead yourself and make this commitment, make an honest list of the time-consuming activities in your life that don't contribute to your future.

1. ____________________
2. ____________________
3. ____________________
4. ____________________
5. ____________________
6. ____________________
7. ____________________
8. ____________________
9. ____________________
10. ____________________

→ Share with Others

Tell yourself and others in your life that you are committed to giving up those activities to focus strictly on your business.

I recommend you sit down with family and friends to share your vision when it's appropriate. You can do this in a ritualistic fashion or casually, but be sure to explain why you are choosing to focus strictly on your business for a year and giving up other activities. Be specific about what you're committing to do and what you have to let go of, and ask for their agreement to hold you accountable.

→ Daily Commitment

Commit to one year of imbalance, and remind yourself daily why you've made this commitment to yourself and your business. Set up a reminder on your phone or another system to connect you daily to your commitment – until reminders aren't necessary and you've internalized this temporary imbalance for massive action.

▶ Learn more about the commitment it takes to build a business to last and the period of imbalance you need in my video course at KeithCallahan.com/BTL.

ACCELERATE

Ten-minute Morning Meditation

Every morning during this module, allow yourself to really get into the *feeling nature* of this period of massive action and temporary imbalance. What happens each day? What do your life, your relationships, your weekends, your evenings, your mornings, your holidays look and feel like without all the activities you listed above? How does it feel as you partner with leaders who you mentor to build their own organizations? What is it like for you as you see your vision come to life? Set a timer for 10 minutes so you can relax fully, and engage all of your senses to explore in your imagination this year of getting the boulder up the hill. That inner experience paves the way for the outer manifestation.

Daily Mantras

As you work through this module, first thing in the morning and last thing at night, repeat to yourself or aloud 10 times:

I am committed to massive action during this period of imbalance,
so my business thrives with or without me.

And 100 times throughout the day, allow this mantra (or another one you prefer) to drive your thinking and your focus.

Ten-minute Evening Reflection

Every evening during this module, set a timer for 10 minutes of reviewing, assessing, and replaying all that went right today. Also take note of one thing that can be improved on. And most important, be in gratitude for all that went well.

At the end of this module, you'll find a habit tracker and space to record your insights and progress, one for each of seven days.

DISCUSS

Possible topics for group meetings around *Module 7, Attracting Leaders* – after the daily practices and action steps have been completed:

- How do you convey to prospective partners that you have the ability to mentor them to achieve their goals?
- What activities have you committed to giving up during this period of imbalance, and why is it worth your while?
- What doubts, setbacks, or obstacles are you encountering?
- How are you keeping yourself focused on your business?

▶ Are you struggling with gaining momentum in your business? Learn more about the importance of getting the boulder over the hill at KeithCallahan.com/BTL.

TRACK

Date ___________ **Habits Check List**

☐ Morning meditation

☐ Morning mantra

☐ Present and follow up on product, service, and/or business opportunity

☐ Daily mantras

☐ Evening reflection

☐ Evening journaling

☐ Evening mantra

What went well?

1. ______________________________________

____

____

____

____

2. ______________________________________

____

____

____

____

3. ______________________________________

____

____

____

____

____

What could I improve? How?

Other notes

TRACK

Date ___________ **Habits Check List**

- ☐ Morning meditation
- ☐ Morning mantra
- ☐ Present and follow up on product, service, and/or business opportunity
- ☐ Daily mantras
- ☐ Evening reflection
- ☐ Evening journaling
- ☐ Evening mantra

What went well?

1. ____________________

____

____

____

____

2. ____________________

____

____

____

____

3. ____________________

____

____

____

____

____

What could I improve? How?

Other notes

TRACK

Date ___________ **Habits Check List**

☐ Morning meditation

☐ Morning mantra

☐ Present and follow up on product, service, and/or business opportunity

☐ Daily mantras

☐ Evening reflection

☐ Evening journaling

☐ Evening mantra

What went well?

1. ____

____

____

____

____

2. ____

____

____

____

____

3. ____

____

____

____

____

____

What could I improve? How?

Other notes

TRACK

Date ___________ **Habits Check List**

- ☐ Morning meditation
- ☐ Daily mantras
- ☐ Morning mantra
- ☐ Evening reflection
- ☐ Present and follow up on product, service, and/or business opportunity
- ☐ Evening journaling
- ☐ Evening mantra

What went well?

1. ______________________________

____

____

____

____

2. ______________________________

____

____

____

____

3. ______________________________

____

____

____

____

____

What could I improve? How?

Other notes

TRACK

Date ___________ **Habits Check List**

☐ Morning meditation

☐ Daily mantras

☐ Morning mantra

☐ Evening reflection

☐ Present and follow up on product, service, and/or business opportunity

☐ Evening journaling

☐ Evening mantra

What went well?

1. ______________________________

____

____

____

____

2. ______________________________

____

____

____

____

3. ______________________________

____

____

____

____

____

What could I improve? How?

Other notes

TRACK

Date ___________ **Habits Check List**

☐ Morning meditation

☐ Morning mantra

☐ Present and follow up on product, service, and/or business opportunity

☐ Daily mantras

☐ Evening reflection

☐ Evening journaling

☐ Evening mantra

What went well?

1. ____

____

____

____

____

2. ____

____

____

____

____

3. ____

____

____

____

____

____

What could I improve? How?

Other notes

TRACK

Date ____________ **Habits Check List**

☐ Morning meditation

☐ Daily mantras

☐ Morning mantra

☐ Evening reflection

☐ Present and follow up on product, service, and/or business opportunity

☐ Evening journaling

☐ Evening mantra

What went well?

1. ____

____

____

____

____

2. ____

____

____

____

____

3. ____

____

____

____

____

____

What could I improve? How?

Other notes

Module 8

IDENTIFYING LEADERS

I was never top of the class at school, but my classmates must have seen potential in me, because my nickname was "Einstein."

— Stephen Hawking

GOAL

To identify potential leaders

→ This module is designed to support you once you have leaders – or potential leaders – on your team.

READ

Once you're able to identify potential leaders, you can start working with them to develop them into the leaders they're meant to be. Recognize that not everybody you sponsor is going to become a leader. In fact, the majority of distributors are never going to get to the next level, no matter what you do.

When you're first getting started, you'll work with anybody who signs up with you as though that person is a leader. Eventually, you want so many people coming into your business that you have to identify the leaders to work with one-on-one and work with everyone else in a group.

Leaders come from all different backgrounds and have all different personality types. However, specific character traits do appear over and over in leaders. They're self-motivated. They're solution-oriented. They're problem solvers. They're competitive. They're usually busy in the rest of their lives. They believe in something bigger than themselves. They're action-oriented. They're dreamers. They're motivated by either inspiration or desperation. And also, they inspire me. In that list of traits, the last two stand out for me as important identifiers.

As I sift for potential leaders, I'm looking for these signs, in order of importance:

1. They're winning challenges.
2. They sign up distributors right away.
3. They implement the trainings.
4. They are coachable.
5. They're helping others.

▶ **Identifying leaders can be difficult. I go through the process in more detail in my video course, available at KeithCallahan.com/BTL.**

DO

→ Are You a Sleeping Giant?

Think back to the story I shared about Hayley in *Build to Last*. She was a "sleeping giant" in my organization who I know intuitively had the ability to build a strong business though she hadn't had any action – yet. When she made the decision to let go of the excuses and fears blocking her growth, she totally took off.

Do you see yourself in Hayley *before* she made the shift? If so, make the decision now to change! It really is just a decision.

▶ I go into exactly how to decide if you or somebody on your team is a sleeping giant in my video course. Available at KeithCallahan.com/BTL.

→ Identifying Leaders

If you have already made the shift and have a working downline and leaders in your organization, make two lists: one of your leaders, another of your potential leaders.

Leaders in my organization

1. ______________________________
2. ______________________________
3. ______________________________
4. ______________________________
5. ______________________________
6. ______________________________
7. ______________________________

8. ____
9. ____
10. ____

Potential leaders in my organization

1. ____
2. ____
3. ____
4. ____
5. ____
6. ____
7. ____
8. ____
9. ____
10. ____

We'll get very detailed about how to mentor your leaders in Module 10.

ACCELERATE

Ten-minute Morning Meditation

Every morning during this module, allow yourself to really get into the *feeling nature* of connecting with a new or existing distributor who has the qualities you want in a team member, someone who has the potential to be one of the five leaders you're looking for, someone you're excited to work with because you get as much out of the relationship as you give. Set a timer for 10 minutes so you can relax fully, and engage all of your senses to explore this scenario in your imagination. That inner experience paves the way for the outer manifestation.

Daily Mantras

As you work through this module, first thing in the morning and last thing at night, repeat to yourself or aloud 10 times:

Working with my leaders, I get as much as I give.

And 100 times throughout the day, allow this mantra to drive your thinking and your focus.

Ten-minute Evening Reflection

Every evening during this module, set a timer for 10 minutes of reviewing, assessing, and replaying all that went right today. Also take note of one thing that can be improved on. And most important, be in gratitude for all that went well.

At the end of this module, you'll find a habit tracker and space to record your insights and progress, one for each of seven days.

DISCUSS

Possible topics for group meetings around *Module 8, Identifying Leaders* – after the daily practices and action steps have been completed:

- Are you a sleeping giant or have you made the shift to a leader of leaders building an organization to last?
- Where are you in the process of identifying leaders?
- What kinds of challenges do you set up for your team members, and are they helping you to identify leaders?
- How are you doing with your personal development plan in general and as it relates to mentoring leaders?

TRACK

Date ___________ **Habits Check List**

☐ Morning meditation

☐ Morning mantra

☐ Present and follow up on product, service, and/or business opportunity

☐ Daily mantras

☐ Evening reflection

☐ Evening journaling

☐ Evening mantra

What went well?

1. ____

____

____

____

____

2. ____

____

____

____

____

3. ____

____

____

____

____

____

What could I improve? How?

Other notes

TRACK

Date ___________ **Habits Check List**

- ☐ Morning meditation
- ☐ Morning mantra
- ☐ Present and follow up on product, service, and/or business opportunity
- ☐ Daily mantras
- ☐ Evening reflection
- ☐ Evening journaling
- ☐ Evening mantra

What went well?

1. ______________________________

____

____

____

____

2. ______________________________

____

____

____

____

3. ______________________________

____

____

____

____

____

What could I improve? How?

Other notes

TRACK

Date ___________ **Habits Check List**

☐ Morning meditation

☐ Morning mantra

☐ Present and follow up on product, service, and/or business opportunity

☐ Daily mantras

☐ Evening reflection

☐ Evening journaling

☐ Evening mantra

What went well?

1. ______________________________

2. ______________________________

3. ______________________________

What could I improve? How?

Other notes

TRACK

Date ____________ **Habits Check List**

- ☐ Morning meditation
- ☐ Morning mantra
- ☐ Present and follow up on product, service, and/or business opportunity
- ☐ Daily mantras
- ☐ Evening reflection
- ☐ Evening journaling
- ☐ Evening mantra

What went well?

1. ____

____

____

____

____

2. ____

____

____

____

____

3. ____

____

____

____

____

____

What could I improve? How?

Other notes

TRACK

Date ___________ **Habits Check List**

☐ Morning meditation

☐ Morning mantra

☐ Present and follow up on product, service, and/or business opportunity

☐ Daily mantras

☐ Evening reflection

☐ Evening journaling

☐ Evening mantra

What went well?

1. ____

____

____

____

____

2. ____

____

____

____

____

3. ____

____

____

____

____

____

What could I improve? How?

Other notes

TRACK

Date ___________ **Habits Check List**

☐ Morning meditation

☐ Morning mantra

☐ Present and follow up on product, service, and/or business opportunity

☐ Daily mantras

☐ Evening reflection

☐ Evening journaling

☐ Evening mantra

What went well?

1. ____

____

____

____

____

2. ____

____

____

____

____

3. ____

____

____

____

____

____

What could I improve? How?

Other notes

TRACK

Date ___________ **Habits Check List**

☐ Morning meditation

☐ Morning mantra

☐ Present and follow up on product, service, and/or business opportunity

☐ Daily mantras

☐ Evening reflection

☐ Evening journaling

☐ Evening mantra

What went well?

1. ______________________________

2. ______________________________

3. ______________________________

What could I improve? How?

Other notes

Module 9
WORKING THE NUMBERS

You don't lead by hitting people over the head – that's assault, not leadership.
— Dwight D. Eisenhower

GOAL
To connect with true leaders
by working the numbers.

→ *This module is designed to support you*
once you have leaders – or potential leaders – on your team.

READ

I see our business as comprised of two "funnels" – one to find distributors and another to identify leaders within those distributors. When you have five true leaders in your downline, you have officially "made it." Eventually your five true leaders are going to develop their own five true leaders. That compounds to a team of 25 leaders. With 25 leaders in your downline, your business is no longer dependent on you. It will grow away from you and continue to grow for years to come.

You are NOT looking for just five people though. Network marketing doesn't work that way. You are looking for five **true leaders**. Your focus, your drive, your activities all point toward finding and developing five true leaders. You have to sift through large volumes of people to find leaders who are hungry to work with you. You may need to talk to 500 people to get one true leader. And you need five leaders in total.

Your skills, energy, momentum, passion, and the speed at which you connect with people about this business will determine WHEN you find your five leaders. It's a numbers game. *Wrap your mind around this.* It's a lot of work, but cultivating five true leaders gives you a business that means freedom in your life!

DO

→ Personal Development Plan

Check in with your personal development plan. What are you working on this week?

→ Maximize the Return on Your Time and Energy

Look at the lists of leaders and potential leaders you made in Module 8. Who are the distributors in your downline that you've been working with diligently yet they're not growing, they're just sucking energy out of you. Make the decision today to LET THEM GO. Stop trying to force something that isn't there. You're not doing yourself or them any favor by continuing to try to motivate them into action.

Instead, use your energy to work your numbers, talk to as many people as you can, and continue to develop yourself as a human being and as a leader until you bring in five true leaders.

→ Visualize Five True Leaders on Your Team

Devote half an hour to visualizing the experience of having found those five true leaders you're looking for and mentoring them powerfully. Imagine they're already on your team. Who are you being when you're mentor to these five leaders? What is your day like? Your week? How do you feel? Write about it in the present tense. E.g., I wake up excited for the first meeting of the day…

____

____

____

____

____

____

____

ACCELERATE

Ten-minute Morning Meditation

Every morning during this module, allow yourself to really get into the *feeling nature* of presenting your opportunity in a way that attracts five true leaders – people with a vision and a dream who will do whatever it takes to succeed. Set a timer for 10 minutes so you can relax fully, and engage all of your senses to explore in your imagination connecting with and working with these five true leaders. That inner experience paves the way for the outer manifestation.

Daily Mantras

As you work through this module, first thing in the morning and last thing at night, repeat to yourself or aloud 10 times:

I'm only looking for five true leaders.

And 100 times throughout the day, allow this mantra to drive your thinking and your focus.

Ten-minute Evening Reflection

Every evening during this module, set a timer for 10 minutes of reviewing, assessing, and replaying all that went right today. Also take note of one thing that can be improved on. And most important, be in gratitude for all that went well.

At the end of this module, you'll find a habit tracker and space to record your insights and progress, one for each of seven days.

DISCUSS

Possible topics for group meetings around *Module 9, Working the Numbers* – after the daily practices and action steps have been completed:

- How are you working each of your funnels?
- How many people do you present your business opportunity to each day?
- How many true leaders are in your downline, and how are you working with them?
- Have you noticed any shift in your own energy as a result of no longer trying to motivate distributors who aren't growing?
- What's working well and what's not working well for you?

▶ BONUS CONTENT: Learn how I used two funnels to find two of my top five leaders, and how you can do the same in my video course at KeithCallahan.com/BTL.

TRACK

Date ___________ **Habits Check List**

☐ Morning meditation

☐ Daily mantras

☐ Morning mantra

☐ Evening reflection

☐ Present and follow up on product, service, and/or business opportunity

☐ Evening journaling

☐ Evening mantra

What went well?

1. ____

____

____

____

____

2. ____

____

____

____

____

3. ____

____

____

____

____

____

What could I improve? How?

Other notes

TRACK

Date ___________ **Habits Check List**

☐ Morning meditation

☐ Morning mantra

☐ Present and follow up on product, service, and/or business opportunity

☐ Daily mantras

☐ Evening reflection

☐ Evening journaling

☐ Evening mantra

What went well?

1. ____

____

____

____

____

2. ____

____

____

____

____

3. ____

____

____

____

____

____

What could I improve? How?

Other notes

TRACK

Date ___________ **Habits Check List**

☐ Morning meditation

☐ Morning mantra

☐ Present and follow up on product, service, and/or business opportunity

☐ Daily mantras

☐ Evening reflection

☐ Evening journaling

☐ Evening mantra

What went well?

1. ____

____

____

____

____

2. ____

____

____

____

____

3. ____

____

____

____

____

____

What could I improve? How?

Other notes

TRACK

Date ____________ **Habits Check List**

☐ Morning meditation

☐ Morning mantra

☐ Present and follow up on product, service, and/or business opportunity

☐ Daily mantras

☐ Evening reflection

☐ Evening journaling

☐ Evening mantra

What went well?

1. ____

____

____

____

____

2. ____

____

____

____

____

3. ____

____

____

____

____

____

What could I improve? How?

Other notes

TRACK

Date ___________ **Habits Check List**

- ☐ Morning meditation
- ☐ Daily mantras
- ☐ Morning mantra
- ☐ Evening reflection
- ☐ Present and follow up on product, service, and/or business opportunity
- ☐ Evening journaling
- ☐ Evening mantra

What went well?

1. ______________________________

____

____

____

____

2. ______________________________

____

____

____

____

3. ______________________________

____

____

____

____

____

What could I improve? How?

Other notes

TRACK

Date ___________ **Habits Check List**

☐ Morning meditation

☐ Morning mantra

☐ Present and follow up on product, service, and/or business opportunity

☐ Daily mantras

☐ Evening reflection

☐ Evening journaling

☐ Evening mantra

What went well?

1. ____________________

2. ____________________

3. ____________________

What could I improve? How?

Other notes

TRACK

Date ___________ **Habits Check List**

☐ Morning meditation

☐ Morning mantra

☐ Present and follow up on product, service, and/or business opportunity

☐ Daily mantras

☐ Evening reflection

☐ Evening journaling

☐ Evening mantra

What went well?

1. ____

2. ____

3. ____

What could I improve? How?

Other notes

Module 10

THE BUILD-TO-LAST MENTORSHIP SYSTEM

Leadership is unlocking people's potential to become better.
— Bill Bradley

GOAL

To begin implementing
your professional mentoring system.

→ This module is designed to support you
once you have leaders – or potential leaders – on your team.

READ

The hours I dedicate to mentoring my leaders fall into two categories:

1. Dedicated days for formal one-on-one mentoring calls during which I connect with the leaders I mentor on a weekly or monthly basis.
2. Small chunks of time on non-mentoring days during which I send supportive, inspirational texts and social media messages, or just pick the phone up and call.

I also work with my leaders as a group in both a weekly video conference and an online social-media forum where we're in communication throughout the day, inspiring each other and sharing leadership principles.

As a professional mentor I'm available via text, phone call, direct message. I'm available if people want to meet face-to-face. For this to be workable for me and my family, I also establish clear boundaries from the start: when I'm working, I'm working, and when I'm off, I'm off.

DO

→ Mentoring Call Flow

At ***KeithCallahan.com/book*** download the template with the flow of my one-on-one mentorship calls and a checklist to keep you on track, and listen to the audio file for further detail of the steps I take when mentoring my leaders.

→ Print and Prepare

Make a list of people in your downline that you want to mentor one-on-one:

1. ______________________________
2. ______________________________
3. ______________________________
4. ______________________________
5. ______________________________
6. ______________________________
7. ______________________________
8. ______________________________
9. ______________________________
10. ______________________________
11. ______________________________
12. ______________________________
13. ______________________________
14. ______________________________
15. ______________________________

Print a copy of my mentorship-calls template for each person, and make notes on their page about potential key performance indicators (KPIs).

Personal recruiting KPI examples:

- Number of new customer sign-ups in a week
- Number of new personally-sponsored distributors in a week
- Number of business presentations in a week
- Number of invites in a week

Team KPI examples:

- Number of new distributors coming into your downline in a week
- Number of rank advancements in your entire downline in a week
- Number of personally-sponsored distributors sponsoring another distributor in a week
- Number of personally-sponsored distributors rank-advancing in a week

→ Schedule Calls

Set up one-on-one mentorship calls with the leaders and potential leaders on your list.

→ Begin Mentoring

Conduct your first mentorship call with each person, setting KPIs for the upcoming week and scheduling your next meeting.

▶ Becoming a mentor can prove challenging at first. If that's your experience, you'll get great value from my *Build to Last* video course. You can get it at KeithCallahan.com/BTL.

ACCELERATE

Ten-minute Morning Meditation

Every morning during this module, allow yourself to really get into the *feeling nature* of being a professional mentor. As you know, on days I work with my leaders, my morning ritual involves getting my mind in the right space. I visualize my calls. I visualize how the day is going to go. I visualize my leaders not as they currently are, but as they can be. Even on non-mentoring days, I still spend time during my morning routine visualizing them at their highest possible level. Give this a try as you work through this module. Set a timer for 10 minutes so you can relax fully, and engage all of your senses. That inner experience paves the way for the outer manifestation.

Daily Mantras

As you work through this module, first thing in the morning and last thing at night, repeat to yourself or aloud 10 times:

I am a professional mentor to my leaders.

And 100 times throughout the day, allow this mantra to drive your thinking and your focus.

Ten-minute Evening Reflection

Every evening during this module, set a timer for 10 minutes of reviewing, assessing, and replaying all that went right today. Also take note of one thing that can be improved on. And most important, be in gratitude for all that went well.

At the end of this module, you'll find a habit tracker and space to record your insights and progress, one for each of seven days.

DISCUSS

Possible topics for group meetings around *Module 10, The Build-to-last Mentorship System* – after the daily practices and action steps have been completed:

- How are you doing on your one-on-one mentorship calls?
- How is the structure – catching up, transition, reviewing and setting new KPIs, and a good ending – working for you and the people you mentor?
- Have you implemented it in your calls?
- Are there pieces you're struggling with?

TRACK

Date ___________ **Habits Check List**

☐ Morning meditation

☐ Morning mantra

☐ Present and follow up on product, service, and/or business opportunity

☐ Daily mantras

☐ Evening reflection

☐ Evening journaling

☐ Evening mantra

What went well?

1. ____________________________________

____

____

____

____

2. ____________________________________

____

____

____

____

3. ____________________________________

____

____

____

____

____

What could I improve? How?

Other notes

TRACK

Date ____________ **Habits Check List**

☐ Morning meditation

☐ Daily mantras

☐ Morning mantra

☐ Evening reflection

☐ Present and follow up on product, service, and/or business opportunity

☐ Evening journaling

☐ Evening mantra

What went well?

1. ____

____

____

____

____

2. ____

____

____

____

____

3. ____

____

____

____

____

____

What could I improve? How?

Other notes

TRACK

Date ___________ **Habits Check List**

- ☐ Morning meditation
- ☐ Daily mantras
- ☐ Morning mantra
- ☐ Evening reflection
- ☐ Present and follow up on product, service, and/or business opportunity
- ☐ Evening journaling
- ☐ Evening mantra

What went well?

1. ____

____

____

____

____

2. ____

____

____

____

____

3. ____

____

____

____

____

____

What could I improve? How?

Other notes

TRACK

Date ____________ **Habits Check List**

☐ Morning meditation

☐ Morning mantra

☐ Present and follow up on product, service, and/or business opportunity

☐ Daily mantras

☐ Evening reflection

☐ Evening journaling

☐ Evening mantra

What went well?

1. ____

____

____

____

____

2. ____

____

____

____

____

3. ____

____

____

____

____

____

What could I improve? How?

Other notes

TRACK

Date ____________ **Habits Check List**

☐ Morning meditation

☐ Morning mantra

☐ Present and follow up on product, service, and/or business opportunity

☐ Daily mantras

☐ Evening reflection

☐ Evening journaling

☐ Evening mantra

What went well?

1. ____

____

____

____

____

2. ____

____

____

____

____

3. ____

____

____

____

____

____

What could I improve? How?

Other notes

TRACK

Date ___________ **Habits Check List**

☐ Morning meditation

☐ Daily mantras

☐ Morning mantra

☐ Evening reflection

☐ Present and follow up on product, service, and/or business opportunity

☐ Evening journaling

☐ Evening mantra

What went well?

1. ____

____

____

____

____

2. ____

____

____

____

____

3. ____

____

____

____

____

____

What could I improve? How?

Other notes

TRACK

Date ___________ **Habits Check List**

☐ Morning meditation

☐ Morning mantra

☐ Present and follow up on product, service, and/or business opportunity

☐ Daily mantras

☐ Evening reflection

☐ Evening journaling

☐ Evening mantra

What went well?

1. ____

____

____

____

____

2. ____

____

____

____

____

3. ____

____

____

____

____

____

What could I improve? How?

Other notes

Module 11
BUILDING TRUST

True leadership stems from individuality that is honestly and sometimes imperfectly expressed... Leaders should strive for authenticity over perfection.
— Sheryl Sandberg

GOAL
To begin building trust with those you mentor through modeling.

→ This module is designed to support you once you have leaders – or potential leaders – on your team.

READ

As leaders of leaders, our real job is developing human beings. We go deep with those we mentor to develop their potential, and to shift how they look at the world and solve problems. We work with their thoughts, their habits, their daily practices. We work to increase their self-esteem. We recognize their dormant potential, and our job is facilitating the emergence of that potential.

To guide someone through this growth process, building trust is imperative.

- Mentor by modeling. Walk your own walk, go through your own stuff, grow into and express your own personal human potential. Be all in. Be vulnerable.
- Be consistent, week after week, month after month, year after year. Trust builds over time.
- Be a mentor first and a friend second.
- Say what those you mentor need to hear, not what they want to hear. If you speak in a nurturing way that pushes them to become more than who they are, they will trust and respect you.

When I start working one-on-one with new people, they're usually focused on questions like "How do I start doing this?" or "What would I say in this situation?" They want to know how to do the *activities* better. What I want to get to, though, is real personal growth. To do that level of work together, we must establish trust.

▶ I further explore trust, belief, and inspiration when mentoring leaders in my video course. Learn more at KeithCallahan.com/BTL.

DO

This is not a one-time action. You must make the following four decisions and commit to growing into each of them:

1. Make the decision to be "all in" on your business.
2. Make the decision to be vulnerable with your leaders.
3. Make the decision to be consistent with your leaders.
4. Make the decision to be honest with your leaders.

Read each decision and commitment, and do a thought download on what arises for you. Is there anything preventing you from 100 percent commitment? Any doubts? Hesitance? Resistance? Fear?

→ I am "all in" on my business.

→ I am vulnerable with my leaders.

→ I am consistent with my leaders.

→ I am honest with my leaders.

____

____

____

____

____

____

____

____

____

____

____

____

Once you shine the light of awareness on any limiting thoughts or beliefs, you can lead yourself (or get help from a colleague or mentor) in order to be fully aligned with these foundational commitments. Remind yourself of them until they become part of who you are.

ACCELERATE

Ten-minute Morning Meditation

Every morning during this module, allow yourself to really get into the *feeling nature* of working with people you mentor to uncover their potential. Bringing out the best in people. Meeting them where they are and seeing where they can go. Helping them see themselves not as they are but as they can be. Practice, in your imagination, speaking truth lovingly to the people you're currently working with. Experience the trust that comes of showing up consistently over time, of sharing your deep belief in your mentee's vision, of being a professional mentor. Set a timer for 10 minutes so you can relax fully, and engage all of your senses to explore this. That inner experience paves the way for the outer manifestation.

Daily Mantras

As you work through this module, first thing in the morning and last thing at night, repeat to yourself or aloud 10 times:

I am a leader of leaders who mentors by modeling.

And 100 times throughout the day, allow this mantra to drive your thinking and your focus.

Ten-minute Evening Reflection

Every evening during this module, set a timer for 10 minutes of reviewing, assessing, and replaying all that went right today. Also take note of one thing that can be improved on. And most important, be in gratitude for all that went well.

At the end of this module, you'll find a habit tracker and space to record your insights and progress, one for each of seven days.

DISCUSS

Possible topics for group meetings around *Module 11, Building Trust* – after the daily practices and action steps have been completed:

- How are you doing in the "mentoring by modeling" department?
- What aspects of mentoring are most challenging for you?
- What aspects of mentoring come naturally to you?
- How do you convey your belief in the people you mentor?

▶ Are you struggling with showing your team that you believe in them? Learn how to go all in on yourself and your team in the *Build to Last* video course – available at KeithCallahan.com/BTL.

TRACK

Date ___________ **Habits Check List**

☐ Morning meditation

☐ Daily mantras

☐ Morning mantra

☐ Evening reflection

☐ Present and follow up on product, service, and/or business opportunity

☐ Evening journaling

☐ Evening mantra

What went well?

1. ____

____

____

____

____

2. ____

____

____

____

____

3. ____

____

____

____

____

____

What could I improve? How?

Other notes

TRACK

Date ___________ **Habits Check List**

☐ Morning meditation

☐ Morning mantra

☐ Present and follow up on product, service, and/or business opportunity

☐ Daily mantras

☐ Evening reflection

☐ Evening journaling

☐ Evening mantra

What went well?

1. ______________________________

____

____

____

____

2. ______________________________

____

____

____

____

3. ______________________________

____

____

____

____

____

What could I improve? How?

Other notes

TRACK

Date ___________ **Habits Check List**

☐ Morning meditation

☐ Morning mantra

☐ Present and follow up on product, service, and/or business opportunity

☐ Daily mantras

☐ Evening reflection

☐ Evening journaling

☐ Evening mantra

What went well?

1. ____

____

____

____

____

2. ____

____

____

____

____

3. ____

____

____

____

____

____

What could I improve? How?

Other notes

TRACK

Date ___________ **Habits Check List**

- ☐ Morning meditation
- ☐ Morning mantra
- ☐ Present and follow up on product, service, and/or business opportunity
- ☐ Daily mantras
- ☐ Evening reflection
- ☐ Evening journaling
- ☐ Evening mantra

What went well?

1. ______________________________

____

____

____

____

2. ______________________________

____

____

____

____

3. ______________________________

____

____

____

____

____

What could I improve? How?

Other notes

TRACK

Date ___________ **Habits Check List**

☐ Morning meditation

☐ Morning mantra

☐ Present and follow up on product, service, and/or business opportunity

☐ Daily mantras

☐ Evening reflection

☐ Evening journaling

☐ Evening mantra

What went well?

1. ____

____

____

____

____

2. ____

____

____

____

____

3. ____

____

____

____

____

____

What could I improve? How?

Other notes

TRACK

Date ___________ **Habits Check List**

☐ Morning meditation

☐ Morning mantra

☐ Present and follow up on product, service, and/or business opportunity

☐ Daily mantras

☐ Evening reflection

☐ Evening journaling

☐ Evening mantra

What went well?

1. ____

____

____

____

____

2. ____

____

____

____

____

3. ____

____

____

____

____

____

What could I improve? How?

Other notes

TRACK

Date ___________ **Habits Check List**

☐ Morning meditation

☐ Daily mantras

☐ Morning mantra

☐ Evening reflection

☐ Present and follow up on product, service, and/or business opportunity

☐ Evening journaling

☐ Evening mantra

What went well?

1. ______________________________

____

____

____

____

2. ______________________________

____

____

____

____

3. ______________________________

____

____

____

____

____

What could I improve? How?

Other notes

Module 12
HELPING MENTEES CROSS BRIDGES

Leaders must be close enough to relate to others,
but far enough ahead to motivate them.
— John Maxwell

GOALS

To get clear about where you are
in your network marketing career and what's required to successfully
cross the next bridge – and to do the same for the leaders you mentor.

→ This module is designed to support you
once you have leaders – or potential leaders – on your team.

READ

Consider the metaphor of a large bridge representing the full arc that begins with bringing in a new customer or distributor and completes when that person has developed into a leader of leaders. The large bridge comprises many small bridges:

- The bridge of becoming a customer
- The bridge of becoming a distributor
- The bridge of becoming a working distributor
- The bridge of entering leadership
- The bridge of becoming a leader of leaders
- The bridge of preparing the leader for the income, responsibility, and recognition coming in

The ultimate goal of a leader who is building to last, is to walk people across their many small bridges as far as they are willing to go. Some will cross one or two bridges, some a few more, and a handful will go all the way with you.

Open doors for your leaders, prop them up. Don't make the mistake of doing the presentation or leading the call yourself because you can currently do it better. Your endgame is developing other leaders. Give them that opportunity.

DO

Succeeding in our industry requires crossing a series of bridges. Knowing where you're at and the next bridge to cross gives you a clear next step in your business growth.

→ What's Your Next Bridge?

Think about yourself and your business. What is the next bridge you need to cross?

____

____

▶ Additional training on how to identify your next step and the next steps of your leaders available at KeithCallahan.com/BTL.

What key skills do you need to acquire and what actions do you need to take to cross that bridge?

____

____

____

____

Reflect on this and record your thoughts, insights, and next steps.

____

____

____

____

→ Next Bridges for Your Leaders

Now think about each of your leaders and potential leaders. What is the next bridge each one of them needs to cross? What are the key skills they need to acquire and actions they need to take?

▶ Go to KeithCallahan.com/BTL to learn how to walk your leaders across bridges.

Name: ______________________________

Next Bridge

____

Key Skills

____
____
____
____
____
____
____
____

Actions

____
____
____
____
____
____
____
____

Name: ____

Next Bridge

____

Key Skills

____

____

____

____

____

____

____

____

Actions

____

____

____

____

____

____

____

____

Name: ______________________________

Next Bridge

____

Key Skills

____
____
____
____
____
____
____
____

Actions

____
____
____
____
____
____
____
____

Name: ______________________________

Next Bridge

____

Key Skills

____

____

____

____

____

____

____

____

Actions

____

____

____

____

____

____

____

____

Name: ______________________________

Next Bridge

____

Key Skills

____

____

____

____

____

____

____

____

Actions

____

____

____

____

____

____

____

____

Name: ______________________________

Next Bridge

____

Key Skills

____
____
____
____
____
____
____
____

Actions

____
____
____
____
____
____
____
____

Name: ______________________________

Next Bridge

____

Key Skills

____

____

____

____

____

____

____

____

Actions

____

____

____

____

____

____

____

____

Name: ____

Next Bridge

____

Key Skills

____
____
____
____
____
____
____
____

Actions

____
____
____
____
____
____
____
____

ACCELERATE

Ten-minute Morning Meditation

Every morning during this module, allow yourself to really get into the *feeling nature* of guiding one of your leaders or potential leaders across the next "bridge." What skills does this person need? Imagine helping him or her develop them. What actions are necessary? Imagine their successful endeavors. Set a timer for 10 minutes so you can relax fully, and engage all of your senses to explore developing your leaders to their fullest potential in your imagination. That inner experience paves the way for the outer manifestation.

Daily Mantras

As you work through this module, first thing in the morning and last thing at night, repeat to yourself or aloud 10 times:

My endgame is developing other leaders.

And 100 times throughout the day, allow this or any other mantra you choose to drive your thinking and your focus.

Ten-minute Evening Reflection

Every evening during this module, set a timer for 10 minutes of reviewing, assessing, and replaying all that went right today. Also take note of one thing that can be improved on. And most important, be in gratitude for all that went well.

At the end of this module, you'll find a habit tracker and space to record your insights and progress, one for each of seven days.

DISCUSS

Possible topics for group meetings around *Module 12, Helping Mentees Cross Bridges* – after the daily practices and action steps have been completed:

- Where are you in the arc of your network marketing career?
- What do you need to cross the next bridge?
- Where are your top five leaders or potential leaders in the process?
- What do they need to cross their next bridges?
- Where are you strongest as a guide and mentor?
- As a mentor, which bridges do you find more challenging to help others cross? Why?

TRACK

Date ___________ **Habits Check List**

☐ Morning meditation

☐ Daily mantras

☐ Morning mantra

☐ Evening reflection

☐ Present and follow up on product, service, and/or business opportunity

☐ Evening journaling

☐ Evening mantra

What went well?

1. ______________________________

____

____

____

____

2. ______________________________

____

____

____

____

3. ______________________________

____

____

____

____

____

What could I improve? How?

Other notes

TRACK

Date ____________ **Habits Check List**

- ☐ Morning meditation
- ☐ Daily mantras
- ☐ Morning mantra
- ☐ Evening reflection
- ☐ Present and follow up on product, service, and/or business opportunity
- ☐ Evening journaling
- ☐ Evening mantra

What went well?

1. ____

____

____

____

____

2. ____

____

____

____

____

3. ____

____

____

____

____

____

What could I improve? How?

Other notes

TRACK

Date ___________ **Habits Check List**

☐ Morning meditation

☐ Daily mantras

☐ Morning mantra

☐ Evening reflection

☐ Present and follow up on product, service, and/or business opportunity

☐ Evening journaling

☐ Evening mantra

What went well?

1. ____

____

____

____

____

2. ____

____

____

____

____

3. ____

____

____

____

____

____

What could I improve? How?

Other notes

TRACK

Date ___________ **Habits Check List**

- ☐ Morning meditation
- ☐ Daily mantras
- ☐ Morning mantra
- ☐ Evening reflection
- ☐ Present and follow up on product, service, and/or business opportunity
- ☐ Evening journaling
- ☐ Evening mantra

What went well?

1. ____

____

____

____

____

2. ____

____

____

____

____

3. ____

____

____

____

____

____

What could I improve? How?

Other notes

TRACK

Date ___________ **Habits Check List**

☐ Morning meditation

☐ Daily mantras

☐ Morning mantra

☐ Evening reflection

☐ Present and follow up on product, service, and/or business opportunity

☐ Evening journaling

☐ Evening mantra

What went well?

1. ____

____

____

____

____

2. ____

____

____

____

____

3. ____

____

____

____

____

____

What could I improve? How?

Other notes

TRACK

Date ___________ **Habits Check List**

☐ Morning meditation

☐ Morning mantra

☐ Present and follow up on product, service, and/or business opportunity

☐ Daily mantras

☐ Evening reflection

☐ Evening journaling

☐ Evening mantra

What went well?

1. ____

2. ____

3. ____

What could I improve? How?

Other notes

TRACK

Date ____________ **Habits Check List**

☐ Morning meditation

☐ Morning mantra

☐ Present and follow up on product, service, and/or business opportunity

☐ Daily mantras

☐ Evening reflection

☐ Evening journaling

☐ Evening mantra

What went well?

1. ____

____

____

____

____

2. ____

____

____

____

____

3. ____

____

____

____

____

____

What could I improve? How?

Other notes

Module 13
LET THEM LEAVE THE NEST

People ask the difference between a leader and a boss.
The leader leads, and the boss drives.
— Theodore Roosevelt

GOAL
To know when to let go
of leaders you have mentored.

→ This module is designed to support you
once you have leaders – or potential leaders – on your team.

READ

As your team starts to grow, don't make the mistake many leaders in this industry make. They create an environment that emphasizes "their" team. That is good for followers, but it's a turn-off to potential leaders. It has enormous negative impact on the growth of a team.

Instead of focusing on being the one leader of the "whole" team, be a leader of leaders who has a team of teams. This business is about duplication of leadership. That's how you build to last. And it takes courage. It takes knowing your worth. It takes the ability to trust others. It takes being a person who doesn't need the spotlight. Ultimately, it takes having enough self-esteem to allow those you mentor to do this business better than you.

When you're working with real leaders, you have to give them room to fly. If you push leaders correctly from the start – encouraging them, giving them opportunities – you'll know when it's time. You'll know when they're ready. If you're aware enough, you'll recognize that there's a certain point at which you're stifling rather than catalyzing a leader's growth.

Once you've got your leaders all the way to the other side of the final bridge and prepared them to handle what's there, it's time to: get out of their way, be available when they need you, continue to partner with them, and enjoy their friendship.

DO

→ Leaders Who Are Ready to Be on Their Own

Think about the leaders in your organization. Are there any you're holding back? Any you need to push out of the nest? If so, make a plan to do so this week. Get these meetings scheduled in your calendar.

→ Leaders Who Have Left the Nest

Think about the leaders who have already gone off on their own. Reach out to them. Let them know you're there if they need anything and you appreciate them.

→ Leaders in Your Organization

Think about the leaders in your organization. Who can you partner with for the next promotion, event, or training?

→ Your Colleagues

Enjoy the time with your leaders!

▶ I share my story of how Liz Hartke "flew the nest" and the rewards of watching my leaders cross the stage in my video course at KeithCallahan.com/BTL.

ACCELERATE

Ten-minute Morning Meditation

Every morning during this module, allow yourself to really get into the *feeling nature* of pride, excitement, and enjoyment that comes with having mentored a leader to the point of their being your equal and maybe even better at this business than you are. Set a timer for 10 minutes so you can relax fully, and engage all of your senses to explore in your imagination the immense satisfaction of being mentor to a leader in this phase of your relationship. That inner experience paves the way for the outer manifestation.

Daily Mantras

As you work through this module, first thing in the morning and last thing at night, repeat to yourself or aloud 10 times:

I celebrate the success of the leaders I've mentored.

And 100 times throughout the day, allow this mantra to drive your thinking and your focus.

Ten-minute Evening Reflection

Every evening during this module, set a timer for 10 minutes of reviewing, assessing, and replaying all that went right today. Also take note of one thing that can be improved on. And most important, be in gratitude for all that went well.

At the end of this module, you'll find a habit tracker and space to record your insights and progress, one for each of seven days.

DISCUSS

Possible topics for group meetings around *Module 13, Let Them Leave the Nest* – after the daily practices and action steps have been completed:

- What is your experience of letting leaders you've mentored "leave the nest"?
- What was your experience of leaving the nest yourself when you outgrew your mentor-mentee relationship, if you have?
- Have you observed leaders – or yourself – standing in the way of others' growth?
- How do you currently demonstrate that you are willing to relinquish the spotlight to the next generation of leaders?
- What next steps have you outlined for yourself toward letting leaders you've mentored leave the nest?

▶ In the end it's all about becoming "an elder" to your leaders. I go into this more deeply in my *Build to Last* course. Learn more at KeithCallahan.com/BTL.

TRACK

Date ____________ **Habits Check List**

☐ Morning meditation

☐ Daily mantras

☐ Morning mantra

☐ Evening reflection

☐ Present and follow up on product, service, and/or business opportunity

☐ Evening journaling

☐ Evening mantra

What went well?

1. ____

____

____

____

____

2. ____

____

____

____

____

3. ____

____

____

____

____

____

What could I improve? How?

Other notes

TRACK

Date ___________ **Habits Check List**

☐ Morning meditation

☐ Morning mantra

☐ Present and follow up on product, service, and/or business opportunity

☐ Daily mantras

☐ Evening reflection

☐ Evening journaling

☐ Evening mantra

What went well?

1. ______________________________

____

____

____

____

2. ______________________________

____

____

____

____

3. ______________________________

____

____

____

____

____

What could I improve? How?

Other notes

TRACK

Date ___________ **Habits Check List**

☐ Morning meditation

☐ Daily mantras

☐ Morning mantra

☐ Evening reflection

☐ Present and follow up on product, service, and/or business opportunity

☐ Evening journaling

☐ Evening mantra

What went well?

1. ____

____

____

____

____

2. ____

____

____

____

____

3. ____

____

____

____

____

____

What could I improve? How?

Other notes

TRACK

Date ___________ **Habits Check List**

☐ Morning meditation

☐ Daily mantras

☐ Morning mantra

☐ Evening reflection

☐ Present and follow up on product, service, and/or business opportunity

☐ Evening journaling

☐ Evening mantra

What went well?

1. ____

____

____

____

____

2. ____

____

____

____

____

3. ____

____

____

____

____

____

What could I improve? How?

Other notes

TRACK

Date ___________ **Habits Check List**

☐ Morning meditation

☐ Daily mantras

☐ Morning mantra

☐ Evening reflection

☐ Present and follow up on product, service, and/or business opportunity

☐ Evening journaling

☐ Evening mantra

What went well?

1. ____

____

____

____

____

2. ____

____

____

____

____

3. ____

____

____

____

____

____

What could I improve? How?

Other notes

TRACK

Date ___________ **Habits Check List**

☐ Morning meditation

☐ Morning mantra

☐ Present and follow up on product, service, and/or business opportunity

☐ Daily mantras

☐ Evening reflection

☐ Evening journaling

☐ Evening mantra

What went well?

1. ____________________

2. ____________________

3. ____________________

What could I improve? How?

Other notes

TRACK

Date ___________ **Habits Check List**

- ☐ Morning meditation
- ☐ Daily mantras
- ☐ Morning mantra
- ☐ Evening reflection
- ☐ Present and follow up on product, service, and/or business opportunity
- ☐ Evening journaling
- ☐ Evening mantra

What went well?

1. ____

____

____

____

____

2. ____

____

____

____

____

3. ____

____

____

____

____

____

What could I improve? How?

Other notes

Made in the USA
Columbia, SC
02 July 2019